Parkinson's Disease Cookbook For Newly Diagnosed

Simple Nutritional Guide and Delicious Recipes to Manage Parkinson's illness at Early Stage

By

Dr. Tate Mandara

Table of Contents

INTRODUCTION... 5

CHAPTER ONE...7

  Understanding Parkinson's Disease...............7

    What is Parkinson's Disease?........................7

    Causes...8

    Common Symptoms....................................10

    Diagnosis..11

    Managing Parkinson's Disease Through Diet. 13

    Foods to Eat and Avoid.................................15

    Tips for Safe and Enjoyable Cooking..............18

CHAPTER TWO...21

  BREAKFAST RECIPES.....................................21

    Blueberry Oatmeal Smoothie....................21

    Blue Majik Pancakes.................................22

    Banana Walnut Muffins.............................24

    Avocado Breakfast Bowl............................25

    Turkey and Cheese Sandwich...................27

    Eggs, Sausage, and Whole Grain Bread.. 28

    Scrambled Tofu with Vegetables...............30

CHAPTER THREE..33

  SNACK RECIPES...33

    Apple Slices with Peanut Butter...............33

    Sweet Potato Noodles with Cashew

    Sauce...34

    Cottage Cheese and Pineapple...............35

    Mushroom and Red Kidney Bean Patties. 36

    Rice Cake with Avocado and Tomato.......37

Beetroot and Cashew Puree.....................38

Almond Butter Energy Balls.....................39

Chocolate Smoothie................................40

CHAPTER FOUR.. **43**

  LUNCH RECIPES.......................................**43**

Quinoa and Vegetable Stir-Fry.................43

Turkey and Avocado Wrap......................45

Lentil Soup with Spinach.........................46

Salmon Salad with Lemon-Dill Dressing...48

Chickpea and Tomato Stew.....................49

Chicken and Vegetable Skewers.............51

Tofu Salad with Sesame Ginger Dressing.52

CHAPTER FIVE...**55**

  DINNER RECIPES......................................**55**

Roast Pumpkin Puree.............................55

Beef and Broccoli Stir-Fry.......................56

Lentil & Vegetable Penne Pasta..............58

Vegetable Curry with Brown Rice.............59

Grilled Chicken with Mango Salsa............61

Eggplant Parmesan................................62

Shrimp and Vegetable Skewers...............64

CHAPTER SIX...**67**

  SOUPS & STEWS.....................................**67**

Carrot and Ginger Soup..........................67

Cauliflower Mash....................................68

Tomato Basil Soup.................................69

Butternut Squash Risotto........................70

Bean and Vegetable Soup.......................71

Creamy Mashed Potatoes.......................72

Spicy Chickpea Stew................................ 73

CHAPTER SEVEN.. **75**

FISH & SEAFOODS.. **75**

Seared Scallops with Spinach..................75

Salmon and Quinoa Bowl........................76

Tuna Salad Lettuce Wraps......................78

Grilled Salmon with Asparagus................79

Seafood Paella..81

Mackerel Salad with Avocado Dressing....82

Lemon Garlic Tilapia................................ 84

CHAPTER EIGHT..**87**

DESSERT RECIPES...................................... **87**

Berry Crisp with Oat Topping................... 87

Banana Oat and Cinnamon Smoothie...... 89

Banana Almond Butter Bites....................90

Mango Smoothie......................................91

Coconut Flour Chocolate Chip Cookies....92

Apple Cinnamon Baked Oatmeal.............94

Apple Crisp..96

7-DAY MEAL PLAN......................................**99**

Day 1..99

Day 2..99

Day 3..99

Day 4.. 100

Day 5.. 100

Day 6.. 100

Day 7.. 101

CONCLUSION..**103**

INTRODUCTION

Justin Alice, a vibrant soul with a passion for life, found herself facing a daunting diagnosis: Parkinson's Disease. Initially overwhelmed by the news, she embarked on a journey to reclaim control of her health. Armed with determination and a thirst for knowledge, Justin delved into research, seeking ways to manage her condition. Discovering the transformative power of nutrition, Justin turned to the Parkinson's Diet Cookbook for guidance. Embracing the diverse array of recipes, she embarked on a culinary adventure, exploring new flavors and nourishing her body from within.

As weeks turned into months, Justin noticed subtle yet profound changes. Her energy levels surged, and moments of stiffness and tremors became less frequent.

Encouraged by these improvements, she pressed on, savoring each meal as a step towards wellness. With time, Justin found herself not just managing her Parkinson's symptoms but thriving. The recipes she once viewed as mere ingredients had become her allies in the fight against her condition. Armed with newfound vitality and a renewed sense of hope, Justin embraced each day with a zest for life, proving that with the right tools and mindset, even the greatest challenges can be overcome.

CHAPTER ONE

Understanding Parkinson's Disease

What is Parkinson's Disease?

Parkinson's Disease is a progressive neurological disorder that affects movement. It occurs when nerve cells in the brain, particularly those producing dopamine, become damaged or die. This deficiency of dopamine leads to various motor symptoms such as tremors, stiffness, and impaired balance and coordination. Currently, Parkinson's Disease affects millions of people worldwide, with a significant number of newly diagnosed cases each year. As a chronic condition, it gradually worsens over time, impacting an individual's quality of life and ability to perform daily activities. Despite its prevalence, there is no cure for Parkinson's Disease. However, various treatments and therapies can help manage symptoms and improve the patient's quality of life. These may include medications, physical therapy, and lifestyle modifications. For those newly diagnosed with Parkinson's Disease, navigating the complexities of the condition can be daunting. However, with proper education, support, and access to resources like specialized cookbooks and dietary guidelines, individuals can take proactive steps to manage their symptoms and maintain their overall well-being.

Causes

The exact cause of Parkinson's Disease remains largely unknown, but it's believed to be a combination of genetic and environmental factors. In newly diagnosed patients, the disease may develop due to a complex interplay of these factors over time. Genetic factors play a role in Parkinson's Disease, with certain gene mutations or variations increasing the risk of developing the condition. However, not all individuals with these genetic predispositions will develop Parkinson's, indicating that other factors are involved.

Environmental factors such as exposure to toxins or chemicals may also contribute to the development of Parkinson's Disease. Studies have suggested that pesticides, herbicides, and other environmental toxins may increase the risk, particularly in individuals with genetic susceptibility.

Additionally, age is a significant risk factor for Parkinson's Disease, with the majority of cases diagnosed in individuals over the age of 60.

However, younger people can also develop the condition, albeit less commonly. Understanding these factors and their interactions may lead to better strategies for prevention and treatment in newly diagnosed patients.

Common Symptoms

In newly diagnosed individuals, Parkinson's Disease commonly manifests through a variety of symptoms affecting movement and other bodily functions. One hallmark symptom is tremors, typically beginning in the hands or fingers and occurring while the individual is at rest. Rigidity or stiffness in the muscles is another prevalent symptom, making movements difficult and sometimes painful. Bradykinesia, or slowness of movement, often accompanies rigidity, leading to a gradual decline in the ability to initiate and execute voluntary movements. Postural instability is also common, increasing the risk of falls and balance problems. Other symptoms may include changes in speech patterns, such as softening or slurring of speech, as well as non-motor symptoms like cognitive impairment, depression, anxiety, and sleep disturbances. While the severity and combination of symptoms vary among individuals, early recognition of these symptoms in newly diagnosed patients allows for timely intervention and management to improve quality of life and slow disease progression.

Diagnosis

Diagnosing Parkinson's disease in newly diagnosed patients involves a thorough assessment by a healthcare professional, typically a neurologist specializing in movement disorders. The diagnosis relies primarily on clinical evaluation, where the healthcare provider observes the patient's symptoms, medical history, and physical examination findings. There is no specific test to definitively diagnose Parkinson's disease, but certain criteria, such as the presence of bradykinesia along with at least one other characteristic symptom like tremors or rigidity, are considered indicative.

Additional tests may be conducted to support the diagnosis and rule out other conditions with similar symptoms. These tests may include brain imaging studies like MRI or CT scans to assess for structural abnormalities, as well as dopamine transporter imaging (DaTscan) to evaluate dopamine levels in the brain.

While diagnosing Parkinson's disease can be challenging, especially in the early stages when symptoms may be subtle or nonspecific, an accurate diagnosis is crucial for initiating appropriate treatment and management strategies tailored to the individual patient's needs. Early diagnosis allows for timely intervention to improve symptoms, slow disease progression, and optimize the patient's quality of life.

Managing Parkinson's Disease Through Diet

Managing Parkinson's disease through diet is an integral part of the overall treatment plan for newly diagnosed patients. While diet alone cannot cure Parkinson's disease, it can play a significant role in managing symptoms, promoting overall health, and potentially slowing disease progression.

A balanced and nutritious diet rich in fruits, vegetables, whole grains, lean proteins, and healthy fats is generally recommended for individuals with Parkinson's.

Certain dietary strategies may be particularly beneficial for managing specific symptoms associated with Parkinson's disease. For example, consuming foods high in antioxidants, such as berries, leafy greens, and nuts, may help reduce oxidative stress and inflammation in the brain, potentially alleviating motor symptoms and protecting against neurodegeneration.

Additionally, some evidence suggests that a Mediterranean-style diet, characterized by high consumption of fruits, vegetables, olive oil, fish, and nuts, may have neuroprotective effects and could benefit individuals with Parkinson's disease. This diet is associated with a lower risk of developing neurodegenerative diseases and may help improve motor function, cognition, and overall quality of life in Parkinson's patients. Adopting a healthy and well-balanced diet can complement other treatment modalities for Parkinson's disease, enhance medication effectiveness, and contribute to better symptom management and overall well-being in newly diagnosed patients.

Foods to Eat and Avoid

For individuals newly diagnosed with Parkinson's disease, making informed dietary choices can significantly impact symptom management and overall well-being. While there is no specific "Parkinson's diet," certain foods can help support brain health, manage symptoms, and optimize medication effectiveness, while others may exacerbate symptoms or interfere with medication.

Foods to Eat:

Fruits and vegetables: Rich in antioxidants, vitamins, and minerals, fruits and vegetables support overall health and may help reduce inflammation and oxidative stress in the brain.

Whole grains: Foods like brown rice, quinoa, oats, and whole wheat bread provide sustained energy and fiber, supporting digestion and gut health.

Lean proteins: Incorporating lean sources of protein such as poultry, fish, beans, lentils, and tofu can help maintain muscle strength and promote satiety.

Healthy fats: Foods high in omega-3 fatty acids, such as fatty fish, flaxseeds, chia seeds, and walnuts, support brain health and may help reduce inflammation.

Water: Staying hydrated is essential for overall health and can help alleviate constipation, a common symptom of

Parkinson's disease.

Foods to Avoid:

Processed foods: Highly processed foods high in sugar, unhealthy fats, and additives may contribute to inflammation and exacerbate symptoms.

Excessive salt: Consuming too much salt can lead to fluid retention and high blood pressure, potentially worsening symptoms such as tremors and dyskinesia.

Saturated and trans fats: Limiting intake of saturated and trans fats found in fried foods, fatty meats, and processed snacks can help reduce inflammation and support heart health.

Caffeine and alcohol: While moderate consumption of caffeine and alcohol may be acceptable for some individuals, excessive intake can interfere with medication effectiveness and exacerbate symptoms such as tremors and insomnia.

By prioritizing nutrient-dense foods and minimizing processed and inflammatory foods, individuals with Parkinson's disease can support their overall health, manage symptoms, and optimize their quality of life. It's essential to consult with your healthcare professional or dietitian to develop a personalized dietary plan tailored to individual needs and preferences.

Tips for Safe and Enjoyable Cooking

When cooking with Parkinson's disease, safety and enjoyment go hand in hand. Here are some tips:

Organize your kitchen: Keep commonly used items within reach to minimize reaching and bending.

Use adaptive tools: Consider utensils with larger grips or weighted bases to enhance stability and control.

Take breaks: Cooking can be physically demanding, so pace yourself and take breaks as needed.

Simplify recipes: Choose recipes with fewer ingredients or steps to make cooking more manageable.

Practice safety measures: Use caution when handling hot items and sharp objects to prevent accidents.

Enjoy the process: Cooking can be therapeutic and enjoyable, so savor the experience and celebrate your culinary creations.

CHAPTER TWO

BREAKFAST RECIPES

Blueberry Oatmeal Smoothie

Serving: One

Cooking Time: 5 minutes

Ingredients:

- 1/2 cup rolled oats
- 1/2 cup blueberries
- 1/2 banana
- 1/2 cup Greek yogurt
- 1/2 cup almond milk
- 1 tablespoon honey

Preparation:

1. Combine rolled oats, blueberries, banana,

2. Greek yogurt, almond milk, and honey in a blender.

3. Blend until smooth and creamy.

4. Pour into a glass and enjoy this nutritious Blueberry Oatmeal Smoothie.

Nutritional Value (Approximate):
Calories: 300, Protein: 15g, Fat: 5g, Fiber: 7g Carbohydrates: 50g

Blue Majik Pancakes

Serving: One
Cooking Time: 15 minutes

Ingredients:
- 1/2 cup almond flour
- 1/2 teaspoon Blue Majik powder
- 1/2 teaspoon baking powder
- 1 egg

- 1/4 cup almond milk
- 1 tablespoon maple syrup

Preparation:

1. In a bowl, mix almond flour, Blue Majik powder, and baking powder.

2. Add the egg, almond milk, and maple syrup to the dry ingredients and mix until smooth.

3. Heat a non-stick pan over medium heat and pour the pancake batter.

4. Cook until bubbles form on the surface, then flip and cook the other side.

5. Serve the Blue Majik Pancakes warm with your favorite toppings.

Nutritional Value (Approximate):

Calories: 280,Protein: 10g, Fat: 15g, Fiber: 5g, Carbohydrates: 20g

Banana Walnut Muffins

Serving: One

Cooking Time: 25 minutes

Ingredients:

- 1 ripe banana, mashed
- 1/4 cup chopped walnuts
- 1/2 cup whole wheat flour
- 1/4 cup oats
- 1 tablespoon honey
- 1/2 teaspoon baking powder
- 1/2 teaspoon cinnamon
- 1 egg

Preparation:

1. Preheat the oven to 350°F (175°C) and line a muffin tin with liners.

2. In a bowl, mix mashed banana, walnuts, whole wheat flour, oats, honey, baking powder, cinnamon, and egg.

3. Spoon the batter into the muffin tin and bake for about 20-25 minutes until golden brown.

4. Allow the Banana Walnut Muffins to cool before enjoying.

Nutritional Value (Approximate):
Calories: 220, Protein: 7g,
Carbohydrates: 30g, Fat: 9g, Fiber: 5g

Avocado Breakfast Bowl

Serving: One
Preparation Time: 10 minutes

Ingredients:
- 1 ripe avocado

•2 eggs

•Salt and pepper to taste

•**Optional toppings**: cherry tomatoes, feta cheese, herbs

Preparation:

1. Cut the avocado in half and remove the pit.

2. Scoop out some of the flesh to create a larger well for the eggs.

3. Crack an egg into each avocado half and season with salt and pepper.

4. Bake in a preheated oven at 375°F (190°C) for about 15 minutes or until the eggs are cooked to your liking.

5. Top with cherry tomatoes, feta cheese, herbs, or your favorite toppings before serving.

Nutritional Value (Approximate):

Calories: 350, Protein: 12g, Fat: 28g, Carbohydrates: 15g, Fiber: 10g

Turkey and Cheese Sandwich

Serving: One
Preparation Time: 10 minutes

Ingredients:
- 2 slices whole-grain bread
- 2 oz sliced turkey breast
- 1 slice cheese (e.g., cheddar or Swiss)
- Lettuce, tomato slices (optional)
- Mustard or mayonnaise (optional)

Preparation:

1. Layer the turkey slices and cheese on one slice of bread.

2. Add lettuce, tomato slices, mustard or mayonnaise if desired.

3. Top with the second slice of bread to create a sandwich.

4. Cut in half if preferred and serve.

Nutritional Value (Approximate):
Calories: 320, Protein: 20g, Fat: 12g
Carbohydrates: 30g, Fiber: 5g

Eggs, Sausage, and Whole Grain Bread

Serving: One
Cooking Time: 15 minutes

Ingredients:
- 2 eggs
- 2 turkey sausage links (or preferred sausage)

•2 slices whole grain bread

•Cooking spray or olive oil for cooking

Preparation:

1. Cook the turkey sausage links in a skillet until browned and cooked through.

2. In the same skillet, cook the eggs to your preference (e.g., scrambled or fried).

3. Toast the whole grain bread slices.

4. Serve the cooked eggs and sausage with the toasted bread for a hearty breakfast.

Nutritional Value (Approximate):
Calories: 400, Protein: 25g, Fat: 20g
Carbohydrates: 30g

Scrambled Tofu with Vegetables

Serving: One

Cooking Time:15 minutes

Ingredients:

- 100g firm tofu
- 1/4 cup diced bell peppers
- 1/4 cup diced onions
- 1/4 cup chopped spinach
- 1/2 teaspoon turmeric
- Salt and pepper to taste
- Cooking spray or olive oil

Preparation:

1. Heat cooking spray or olive oil in a pan over medium heat.

2. Add diced onions and bell peppers; sauté until softened.

3. Crumble tofu into the pan; add turmeric, salt, pepper; cook for about five minutes.

4. Add chopped spinach; cook until wilted.

5. Serve hot as a nutritious breakfast option.

Nutritional Value (Approximate):

Calories:250, Protein:15g, Fat: 15g

Carbohydrates:10g

CHAPTER THREE

SNACK RECIPES

Apple Slices with Peanut Butter

Serving: One

Preparation Time: 5 minutes

Ingredients:
- 1 medium apple, sliced
- 2 tablespoons peanut butter

Preparation:

1. Slice the apple into wedges.

2. Dip the apple slices in peanut butter.

3. Enjoy this simple and nutritious snack.

Nutritional Value (Approximate):

Calories: 200, Protein: 6g, Fat: 10g,
 Fiber: 5g, Carbohydrates: 25g

Sweet Potato Noodles with Cashew Sauce

Serving: One

Cooking Time: 20 minutes

Ingredients:

- 1 small sweet potato, spiralized into noodles
- 1/4 cup cashews, soaked
- 1/2 cup water
- Salt and pepper to taste

Preparation:

1. Spiralize the sweet potato into noodles.

2. Blend soaked cashews with water to make a creamy sauce.

3. Sauté sweet potato noodles until tender, then toss with cashew sauce.

4. Season with salt and pepper before serving.

Nutritional Value (Approximate):
Calories: 250, Protein: 8g, Fat: 12g,
Fiber: 6g, Carbohydrates: 30g

Cottage Cheese and Pineapple

Serving: One
Preparation Time: 5 minutes

Ingredients:
- 1/2 cup cottage cheese
- 1/2 cup fresh pineapple chunks

Preparation:

1. Place cottage cheese in a bowl.

2. Top with fresh pineapple chunks.

3. Enjoy this protein-rich and refreshing snack.

Nutritional Value (Approximate):
Calories: 150, Protein: 12g, Fat: 5g
Carbohydrates: 15g,

Mushroom and Red Kidney Bean Patties

Serving: One
Cooking Time: Approximately 20 minutes

Ingredients:
- 1/2 cup mushrooms, chopped
- 1/2 cup red kidney beans, mashed
- 1/4 cup breadcrumbs
- 1/4 teaspoon garlic powder
- Salt and pepper to taste

Preparation:

1. In a bowl, mix mushrooms, red kidney beans, breadcrumbs, garlic powder, salt, and pepper.

2. Form the mixture into patties.

3. Cook in a pan until golden brown on both sides.

Nutritional Value: Protein: 8g, Carbs: 20g, Fat: 3g, Calories: 140

Rice Cake with Avocado and Tomato

Serving: One

Cooking Time: Approximately 10 minutes

Ingredients:

● 1 rice cake

- 1/2 avocado, sliced
- 1/2 tomato, sliced

Preparation:

1. Place avocado slices on the rice cake.

2. Top with tomato slices.

Nutritional Value: Protein: 2g, Carbs: 15g, Fat: 10g, Calories: 150

Beetroot and Cashew Puree

Serving: One

Cooking Time: Approximately 15 minutes

Ingredients:

- 1 small beetroot, cooked and peeled
- Handful of cashews
- Salt to taste

Preparation:

1. Blend cooked beetroot and cashews until smooth.

2. Add salt to taste.

Nutritional Value: Protein: 4g, Carbs: 20g, Fat: 8g, Calories:180

Almond Butter Energy Balls

Serving: One

Preparation Time: Approximately 15 minutes

Ingredients:
- 1/4 cup almond butter
- 2 tablespoons honey
- 1/2 cup oats
- Chia seeds for coating (optional)

Preparation:

1. Mix almond butter, honey, and oats in a bowl.

2. Roll into small balls and coat with chia seeds if desired.

Nutritional Value: Protein:5g, Carbs:25g, Fat:10g, Calories:200

Chocolate Smoothie

Serving: One

Preparation Time: Approximately 5 minutes

Ingredients:-

- 1 banana
- 1 tablespoon cocoa powder
- 1/2 cup almond milk
- Ice cubes (optional)

Preparation:

1. Blend banana, cocoa powder, and almond milk until smooth.

2. Add ice cubes if desired.

Nutritional Value: Protein:3g, Carbs:30g, Fat:3g, Calories:150

CHAPTER FOUR

LUNCH RECIPES

Quinoa and Vegetable Stir-Fry

Serving: One

Cooking Time: Approximately 20 minutes

Ingredients:

- 1/2 cup cooked quinoa
- 1 cup mixed vegetables (bell peppers, broccoli, carrots)
- 1 tablespoon olive oil
- 1 clove garlic, minced
- Soy sauce or tamari to taste

Preparation:

1. Heat olive oil in a pan over medium heat.

2. Add minced garlic and sauté until fragrant.

3. Add mixed vegetables and stir-fry until tender-crisp.

4. Add cooked quinoa and soy sauce, stir well to combine.

5. Cook for a few more minutes until heated through. Serve this nutritious quinoa and vegetable stir-fry hot.

Nutritional Value (Approximate):
Calories: 300, Carbohydrates: 40g, Fat: 12g
Protein: 8g, Fiber: 6g, Sugar: 5g

Turkey and Avocado Wrap

Serving: One

Preparation Time: Approximately 10 minutes

Ingredients:

- 2 slices of turkey breast
- 1/4 avocado, sliced
- 1 whole wheat or gluten-free wrap
- Handful of spinach leaves
- Mustard or hummus for spreading

Preparation:

1. Lay the wrap flat and spread mustard or hummus.

2. Layer turkey slices, avocado, and spinach on the wrap.

3. Roll up the wrap tightly and slice in half if desired. Enjoy this simple and satisfying turkey and avocado wrap.

Nutritional Value (Approximate):
Calories: 250, Carbohydrates: 20g, Fat: 8g
Protein: 15g, Fiber: 6g, Sugar: 2g

Lentil Soup with Spinach

Serving: One
Cooking Time: Approximately 30 minutes

Ingredients:
- 1/2 cup cooked lentils
- 1 cup fresh spinach
- 1 carrot, diced
- 1 celery stalk, chopped
- 1/2 onion, diced
- 2 cups vegetable broth
- 1/2 teaspoon cumin
- Salt and pepper to taste

Preparation:

1. In a pot, sauté onion, carrot, and celery until softened.

2. Add cooked lentils, vegetable broth, cumin, salt, and pepper.

3. Simmer for about 20 minutes.

4. Add fresh spinach and cook until wilted.

5. Serve this hearty lentil soup hot.

Nutritional Value (Approximate):

Calories: 250, Carbohydrates: 40g, Fat:2g

Protein: 15g, Fiber: 12g, Sugar: 5g

Salmon Salad with Lemon-Dill Dressing

Serving: One

Preparation Time: Approximately 15 minutes

Ingredients:

- 4 oz cooked salmon, flaked
- 1 cup mixed greens
- 1/4 cucumber, sliced
- 1/4 red onion, thinly sliced
- 1 tablespoon lemon juice
- 1/2 tablespoon olive oil
- Fresh dill for garnish
- Salt and pepper to taste

Preparation:

1. In a bowl, combine mixed greens, cucumber, and red onion.

2. Top with flaked salmon.

3. In a separate bowl, whisk together lemon juice, olive oil, salt, and pepper to make the dressing.

4. Drizzle the dressing over the salad.

5. Garnish with fresh dill before serving.

Nutritional Value (Approximate):
Calories: 300, Carbohydrates: 10g, Fat: 15g
Protein: 25g, Fiber: 5g, Sugar: 3g

Chickpea and Tomato Stew

Serving: One

Cooking Time: Approximately 25 minutes

Ingredients:
- 1/2 cup cooked chickpeas
- 1/2 cup diced tomatoes

- 1/4 onion, chopped
- 1 clove garlic, minced
- 1/2 teaspoon cumin
- 1/2 teaspoon paprika
- Salt and pepper to taste

Preparation:

1. In a pot, sauté onion and garlic until fragrant.

2. Add diced tomatoes, chickpeas, cumin, paprika, salt, and pepper.

2. Simmer for about 15-20 minutes.

3. Adjust seasoning if needed.

4. Serve this flavorful chickpea and tomato stew hot.

Nutritional Value (Approximate):

Calories: 220, Carbohydrates: 35g, Fat: 5g

Protein: 10g, Fiber: 10g, Sugar: 5g

Chicken and Vegetable Skewers

Serving: One

Cooking Time: Approximately 20 minutes

Ingredients:

- 4 oz chicken breast, cubed
- 1/2 bell pepper, cut into chunks
- 1/2 zucchini, sliced
- 1 tablespoon olive oil
- Lemon wedges for garnish
- Salt, pepper, & your choice of herbs/spices

Preparation:

1. Thread chicken cubes, bell pepper chunks, and zucchini slices onto skewers.

2. Brush with olive oil and season with salt, pepper, and herbs/spices.

3. Grill or bake the skewers until the chicken is cooked through.

4. Serve with lemon wedges on the side.

Nutritional Value (Approximate):
Calories: 280, Carbohydrates: 10g, Fat: 12g
Protein: 30g, Fiber: 3g, Sugar: 5g

Tofu Salad with Sesame Ginger Dressing

Serving: One

Preparation Time: Approximately 15 minutes

Ingredients:
- 1/2 block of firm tofu, cubed
- 1 cup mixed salad greens
- 1/4 cup shredded carrots
- 1/4 cup sliced cucumber
- 1 tablespoon sesame seeds

- 1 tablespoon soy sauce
- 1/2 tablespoon rice vinegar
- 1/2 tablespoon sesame oil
- 1/2 teaspoon grated ginger

Preparation:

1. In a bowl, combine tofu, mixed salad greens, shredded carrots, and sliced cucumber.

2. In a separate bowl, whisk together soy sauce, rice vinegar, sesame oil, and grated ginger to make the dressing.

3. Drizzle the dressing over the salad and tofu.

4. Sprinkle sesame seeds on top before serving.

Nutritional Value (Approximate):

Calories: 250, Carbohydrates: 15g, Fat: 15g

Protein: 15g, Fiber: 5g, Sugar: 3g

CHAPTER FIVE

DINNER RECIPES

Roast Pumpkin Puree

Serving: One

Cooking Time: Approximately 45 minutes

Ingredients:
- 1 cup diced pumpkin
- 1 tablespoon olive oil
- 1/2 teaspoon cinnamon
- Salt and pepper to taste

Preparation:

1. Preheat the oven to 400°F (200°C).

2. Toss diced pumpkin with olive oil, cinnamon, salt, and pepper.

3. Roast in the oven for about 30-40 minutes until tender.

4. Blend the roasted pumpkin until smooth to make the puree.

5. Serve this creamy and flavorful roast pumpkin puree.

Nutritional Value (Approximate):
Calories: 150, Carbohydrates: 20g, Fat: 8g
Protein: 2g, Fiber: 5g, Sugar: 5g

Beef and Broccoli Stir-Fry

Serving: One
Cooking Time: Approximately 20 minutes

Ingredients:
- 4 oz beef strips
- 1 cup broccoli florets
- 1/2 bell pepper, sliced

- 1 clove garlic, minced
- 1 tablespoon soy sauce
- 1/2 tablespoon honey
- 1/2 tablespoon sesame oil

Preparation:

1. Heat sesame oil in a pan over medium-high heat.

2. Add minced garlic and beef strips, stir-fry until browned.

3. Add broccoli, bell pepper, soy sauce, and honey.

4. Cook for a few minutes until vegetables are tender-crisp.

5. Serve this savory beef and broccoli stir-fry hot.

Nutritional Value (Approximate):

Calories: 300, Carbohydrates: 15g, Fat: 15g

Protein: 25g, Fiber: 5g, Sugar: 8g

Lentil & Vegetable Penne Pasta

Serving: One

Cooking Time: Approximately 30 minutes

Ingredients:

- 1/2 cup cooked lentils
- 1/2 cup cooked whole wheat penne pasta
- 1/2 cup diced tomatoes
- 1/4 cup chopped spinach
- 1/4 onion, diced
- 1 clove garlic, minced
- 1/2 tablespoon olive oil
- Italian seasoning, salt, and pepper to taste

Preparation:

1. In a pan, sauté onion and garlic in olive oil until softened.

2. Add diced tomatoes and chopped spinach, cook until spinach wilts.

3. Stir in cooked lentils, cooked penne pasta, Italian seasoning, salt, and pepper.

4. Cook for a few more minutes until heated through. Serve this wholesome lentil & vegetable penne pasta hot.

Nutritional Value (Approximate):
Calories: 300, Carbohydrates: 45g, Fat: 8g
Protein: 15g, Fiber: 10g, Sugar: 5g

Vegetable Curry with Brown Rice

Serving: One

Cooking Time: Approximately 40 minutes

Ingredients:

- 1/2 cup mixed vegetables (bell peppers, carrots, peas)
- 1/4 cup diced potatoes
- 1/4 cup diced tomatoes
- 1/4 onion, chopped
- 1/2 cup cooked brown rice
- 1/2 cup coconut milk
- 1/2 tablespoon curry powder
- Salt and pepper to taste

Preparation:

1. In a pot, sauté onion until translucent. Add mixed vegetables, potatoes, diced tomatoes, curry powder, salt, and pepper.

2. Pour in coconut milk and simmer until vegetables are tender.

3. Serve the vegetable curry over cooked brown rice.

Nutritional Value (Approximate):

Calories: 350, Carbohydrates: 50g, Fat: 15g
Protein: 8g, Fiber: 8g, Sugar: 5g

Grilled Chicken with Mango Salsa

Serving: One

Cooking Time: Approximately 25 minutes

Ingredients:

- 4 oz chicken breast
- 1/2 mango, diced
- 1/4 red bell pepper, diced
- 1/4 red onion, diced
- 1 tablespoon lime juice
- Fresh cilantro for garnish
- Salt and pepper to taste

Preparation:

1. Season the chicken breast with salt and pepper.

2. Grill the chicken until cooked through.

3. In a bowl, mix diced mango, red bell pepper, red onion, lime juice, salt, and pepper to make the salsa.

4. Serve the grilled chicken topped with mango salsa. Garnish with fresh cilantro.

Nutritional Value (Approximate):
Calories: 280, Carbohydrates: 20g, Fat: 8g
Protein: 30g, Fiber: 4g, Sugar: 15g

Eggplant Parmesan

Serving: One

Cooking Time: Approximately 45 minutes

Ingredients:
- 1/2 eggplant, sliced
- 1/4 cup marinara sauce
- 1/4 cup shredded mozzarella cheese

●1 tablespoon grated Parmesan cheese

●1/4 teaspoon dried oregano

●1/4 teaspoon garlic powder

●Fresh basil for garnish

Preparation:

1. Preheat the oven to 375°F (190°C).

2. Layer sliced eggplant in a baking dish, top with marinara sauce, mozzarella, Parmesan, oregano, and garlic powder.

3. Bake for about 30-35 minutes until the cheese is bubbly and golden.

4. Garnish with fresh basil before serving this comforting eggplant Parmesan.

Nutritional Value (Approximate):

Calories: 250, Carbohydrates: 20g, Fat: 15g
Protein: 10g, Fiber: 8g, Sugar: 10g

Shrimp and Vegetable Skewers

Serving: One

Cooking Time: Approximately 20 minutes

Ingredients:

- 4 large shrimp, peeled and deveined
- 1/2 zucchini, sliced
- 1/2 bell pepper, cut into chunks
- 1/4 onion, cut into wedges
- 1 tablespoon olive oil
- Lemon wedges for garnish
- Salt, pepper, & your choice of herbs/spices

Preparation:

1. Thread shrimp, zucchini slices, bell pepper chunks, and onion wedges onto skewers.

2. Brush with olive oil and season with salt, pepper, and herbs/spices.

3. Grill or bake the skewers until the shrimp is cooked through.

4. Serve with lemon wedges on the side.

Nutritional Value (Approximate):
Calories: 200, Carbohydrates: 10g, Fat: 10g, Protein: 20g, Fiber: 3g, Sugar: 5g

CHAPTER SIX

SOUPS & STEWS

Carrot and Ginger Soup

Serving: One

Cooking Time: Approximately 30 minutes

Ingredients:

- 1 dessert spoon olive oil
- 1 large onion, chopped
- 6 medium carrots, chopped
- 100g red lentils
- 1 litre vegetable or chicken stock
- 2 in root ginger, peeled and grated (about 1 tsp)
- Juice and zest of 1/2 orange

Preparation:

1. Heat the oil in a pan, add onion, cook until translucent.

2. Add carrots, lentils, and stock. Simmer for 15 minutes.

3. Remove from heat, add ginger, orange juice, and zest.

4. Blend until smooth.

Nutritional Value: Protein: 8g, Carbs: 30g, Fat: 5g, Calories: 200

Cauliflower Mash

Serving: One

Cooking Time: Approximately 20 minutes

Ingredients:
- Cauliflower florets

- Vegetable broth
- Salt and pepper to taste

Preparation:

1. Steam cauliflower until tender.

2. Blend with vegetable broth until smooth.

3. Season with salt and pepper.

Nutritional Value: Protein:4g, Carbs:15g, Fat:3g, Calories:120

Tomato Basil Soup

Serving: One

Cooking Time: Approximately 25 minutes

Ingredients:-

- Tomatoes, diced
- Fresh basil
- Vegetable broth - Garlic - Olive oil

Preparation:

1. Sauté garlic in olive oil until fragrant.

2. Add tomatoes and vegetable broth, simmer until tomatoes are soft.

3. Blend with fresh basil.

Nutritional Value: Protein :5g, Carbs :20g, Fat :4g,Calories :150

Butternut Squash Risotto

Serving: One

Cooking Time: Approximately 40 minutes

Ingredients:-

- Butternut squash cubes
- Arborio rice
- Vegetable broth
- Parmesan cheese

Preparation:

1. Sauté butternut squash cubes until tender

2. Add Arborio rice and vegetable broth gradually until cooked.

3. Stir in Parmesan cheese before serving.

Nutritional Value:Protein :6g,Carbs :30g, Fat :8g,Calories :220

Bean and Vegetable Soup

Serving: One

Cooking Time: Approximately 30 minutes

Ingredients:

- Assorted beans (kidney beans, chickpeas)
- Mixed vegetables (carrots, celery)
- Vegetable broth

Preparation:

1. Cook beans and vegetables in vegetable broth until tender.

2. Season as desired before serving.

Nutritional Value: Protein :10g,Carbs :25g, Fat :3g,Calories :180

Creamy Mashed Potatoes

Serving: One

Cooking Time: Approximately 25 minutes

Ingredients:
- Potatoes, peeled and cubed
- Milk (or dairy-free alternative)
- Butter (or vegan butter)
- Salt and pepper to taste

Preparation:

1. Boil potatoes until soft.

2. Mash with milk, butter, salt, and pepper until creamy.

Nutritional Value: Protein :4g,Carbs :20g, Fat :5g,Calories :150

Spicy Chickpea Stew

Serving: One

Cooking Time: Approximately 35 minutes

Ingredients:
- Chickpeas, cooked
- Bell peppers, diced
- Onion and garlic for flavoring
- Spices (cumin, paprika)

Preparation:

1. Sauté onion and garlic until fragrant.

2. Add chickpeas, bell peppers, and spices; simmer until flavors meld.

Nutritional Value:Protein :12g,Carbs :25g, Fat :5g,Calories :200

CHAPTER SEVEN

FISH & SEAFOODS

Seared Scallops with Spinach

Serving: One

Cooking Time: Approximately 15 minutes

Ingredients:
- 4 large scallops
- 1 cup fresh spinach
- 1 tablespoon olive oil
- Salt and pepper to taste

Preparation:

1. Heat olive oil in a skillet over medium-high heat.

2. Season scallops with salt and pepper, then sear for about 2-3 minutes on each side until golden brown.

3. Serve the scallops over a bed of fresh spinach.

Nutritional Value (Approximate):
Calories: 150, Carbohydrates: 3g, Fat: 7g
Protein: 20g, Fiber: 2g, Sugar: 1g

Salmon and Quinoa Bowl

Serving: One
Cooking Time: Approximately 20 minutes

Ingredients:
- 4 oz salmon fillet
- 1/2 cup cooked quinoa
- 1/2 cup steamed asparagus
- Lemon wedges for garnish
- Salt and pepper to taste

Preparation:

1. Season the salmon with salt and pepper, then bake or grill until cooked through.

2. Arrange cooked quinoa and steamed asparagus in a bowl.

3. Place the cooked salmon on top.

4. Garnish with lemon wedges before serving.

Nutritional Value (Approximate):

Calories: 300, Carbohydrates: 20g, Fat: 12g, Protein: 25g, Fiber: 5g, Sugar: 2g

Tuna Salad Lettuce Wraps

Serving: One

Preparation Time: Approximately 10 minutes

Ingredients:
- 1/2 can of tuna, drained
- 1 tablespoon Greek yogurt
- 1 tablespoon diced celery
- 1 tablespoon diced red onion
- Lettuce leaves for wrapping

Preparation:

1. In a bowl, mix tuna, Greek yogurt, celery, and red onion until well combined.

2. Spoon the tuna salad mixture onto lettuce leaves.

3. Roll up the lettuce leaves to create wraps.

4. Enjoy these light and flavorful tuna salad lettuce wraps.

Nutritional Value (Approximate):
Calories: 150, Carbohydrates: 5g, Fat: 8g
Protein: 15g, Fiber: 2g, Sugar: 2g

Grilled Salmon with Asparagus

Serving: One
Cooking Time: Approximately 15 minutes

Ingredients:
- 4 oz salmon fillet
- 1/2 cup asparagus spears
- 1 tablespoon olive oil
- Lemon slices for garnish
- Salt and pepper to taste

Preparation:

1. Preheat a grill or grill pan over medium-high heat.

2. Brush salmon and asparagus with olive oil, then season with salt and pepper.
3. Grill the salmon for about 4-5 minutes per side and the asparagus for 3-4 minutes until tender.

4. Serve the grilled salmon with asparagus, garnished with lemon slices.

Nutritional Value (Approximate):
Calories: 250, Carbohydrates: 5g, Fat: 15g
Protein: 25g, Fiber: 3g, Sugar: 2g

Seafood Paella

Serving: One

Cooking Time: Approximately 30 minutes

Ingredients:

- 1/4 cup cooked shrimp
- 1/4 cup cooked mussels
- 1/2 cup cooked brown rice
- 1/4 cup diced bell peppers
- 1/4 cup diced tomatoes
- 1/4 teaspoon paprika
- 1/4 teaspoon saffron (optional)
- Salt and pepper to taste

Preparation:

1. In a skillet, sauté bell peppers and tomatoes until softened.

2. Add cooked shrimp, mussels, brown rice, paprika, saffron, salt, and pepper.

3. Cook for a few minutes until heated through.

4. Serve this flavorful seafood paella hot.

Nutritional Value (Approximate):
Calories: 300, Carbohydrates: 35g, Fat: 8g
Protein: 20g, Fiber: 5g, Sugar: 3g

Mackerel Salad with Avocado Dressing

Serving: One

Preparation Time: Approximately 15 minutes

Ingredients:
- 1/2 can of mackerel, drained
- 1/2 avocado
- 1 tablespoon Greek yogurt
- 1 tablespoon lemon juice

●Salt and pepper to taste

Preparation:

1. In a bowl, mash the avocado and mix with Greek yogurt, lemon juice, salt, and pepper to make the dressing.

2. Flake the mackerel and toss with the avocado dressing.

3. Serve this mackerel salad as a light and flavorful meal.

Nutritional Value (Approximate):
Calories: 250, Carbohydrates: 10g, Fat: 15g
Protein: 20g, Fiber: 6g, Sugar: 2g

Lemon Garlic Tilapia

Serving: One

Cooking Time: Approximately 20 minutes

Ingredients:
- 1 tilapia fillet
- 1 clove garlic, minced
- 1 tablespoon lemon juice
- 1 tablespoon olive oil
- Fresh parsley for garnish
- Salt and pepper to taste

Preparation:

1. Preheat the oven to 400°F (200°C).

2. Place the tilapia fillet on a baking sheet lined with parchment paper.

3. In a small bowl, mix garlic, lemon juice, olive oil, salt, and pepper.

4. Brush the mixture over the tilapia.

5. Bake for about 15-18 minutes until the fish is cooked through.

6. Garnish with fresh parsley before serving.

Nutritional Value (Approximate):
Calories: 200, Carbohydrates: 2g, Fat: 10g
Protein: 25g

CHAPTER EIGHT

DESSERT RECIPES

Berry Crisp with Oat Topping

Serving: One

Cooking Time: Approximately 30 minutes

Ingredients:
- 1/2 cup mixed berries
- 1 tablespoon oats
- 1 tablespoon almond flour
- 1 tablespoon chopped nuts (optional)
- 1 tablespoon maple syrup
- 1/2 tablespoon coconut oil

Preparation:

1. Preheat the oven to 350°F (180°C).

2. In a small bowl, mix the berries with half of the maple syrup and place them in a ramekin.

3. In another bowl, combine oats, almond flour, chopped nuts, the remaining maple syrup, and coconut oil until crumbly.

4. Sprinkle the oat topping over the berries.

5. Bake for about 20-25 minutes until the topping is golden brown and the berries are bubbling.

6. Let it cool slightly before serving.

Nutritional Value (Approximate):
Calories: 250, Carbohydrates: 30g, Fat: 13g
Protein: 4g, Fiber: 5g, Sugar: 15g

Banana Oat and Cinnamon Smoothie

Serving: One

Cooking Time: Approximately 5 minutes

Ingredients:

- 1 ripe banana
- 1/2 cup oats
- 1/2 teaspoon cinnamon
- 1 cup almond milk
- 1 tablespoon honey (optional)

Preparation:

1. Blend the banana, oats, cinnamon, almond milk, and honey until smooth.

2. Pour into a glass and enjoy immediately.

Nutritional Value (Approximate):

Calories: 300, Carbohydrates: 55g, Protein: 7g, Fat: 6g, Fiber: 8g, Sugar: 20g

Banana Almond Butter Bites

Serving: One

Preparation Time: Approximately 10 minutes

Ingredients:
- 1 ripe banana
- 1 tablespoon almond butter
- 1 tablespoon chopped almonds

Preparation:

1. Slice the banana into rounds.

2. Spread almond butter on each banana slice.

3. Sprinkle chopped almonds on top. Enjoy as a quick and satisfying dessert.

Nutritional Value (Approximate):

Calories: 150, Carbohydrates: 20g, Protein: 4g, Fat: 8g, Fiber: 3g, Sugar: 10g

Mango Smoothie

Serving: One

Preparation Time: Approximately 5 minutes

Ingredients:
- 1 ripe mango, peeled and diced
- 1/2 cup Greek yogurt
- 1/4 cup coconut milk
- 1 tablespoon honey (optional)

Preparation:

1. Blend the mango, Greek yogurt, coconut milk, and honey until smooth.

2. Pour into a glass and enjoy this refreshing mango smoothie.

Nutritional Value (Approximate):

Calories: 220, Carbohydrates: 40g, Protein: 8g, Fat: 5g, Fiber: 3g, Sugar: 35g

Coconut Flour Chocolate Chip Cookies

Serving: One

Cooking Time: Approximately 15 minutes

Ingredients:

- 2 tablespoons coconut flour
- 1 tablespoon coconut oil, melted
- 1 tablespoon maple syrup
- 1/4 teaspoon vanilla extract
- 1 tablespoon dark chocolate chips

Preparation:

1. Preheat the oven to 350°F (180°C) and line a baking sheet with parchment paper.

2. In a bowl, mix coconut flour, coconut oil, maple syrup, and vanilla extract until well combined.

3. Fold in the chocolate chips.

4. Form the dough into small cookies and place them on the baking sheet.

5. Bake for about 10-12 minutes until golden brown.

6. Allow to cool before enjoying these delicious coconut flour chocolate chip cookies.

Nutritional Value (Approximate):
Calories: 200, Carbohydrates: 20g, Fat: 12g
Protein: 3g, Fiber: 5g, Sugar: 10g

Apple Cinnamon Baked Oatmeal

Serving: One
Cooking Time: Approximately 25 minutes

Ingredients:
- 1/2 cup rolled oats
- 1/2 apple, diced
- 1/2 teaspoon cinnamon
- 1/4 teaspoon nutmeg
- 1/2 cup almond milk
- 1 tablespoon maple syrup

Preparation:

1. Preheat the oven to 350°F (180°C) and grease a small baking dish.

2. In a bowl, mix oats, diced apple, cinnamon, nutmeg, almond milk, and maple syrup.

3. Pour the mixture into the baking dish.

4. Bake for about 20-25 minutes until the top is golden brown and set.

5. Allow to cool slightly before serving this comforting apple cinnamon baked oatmeal.

Nutritional Value (Approximate):

Calories: 280, Carbohydrates: 45g, Fat: 7g

Protein: 6g, Fiber: 7g, Sugar: 20g

Apple Crisp

Serving: One

Cooking Time: Approximately 30 minutes

Ingredients:
- 1/2 apple, sliced
- 1 tablespoon almond flour
- 1 tablespoon oats
- 1 tablespoon chopped walnuts
- 1 tablespoon maple syrup
- 1/2 tablespoon coconut oil

Preparation:

1. Preheat the oven to 350°F (180°C).

2. In a bowl, mix apple slices with half of the maple syrup and place them in a ramekin.

3. In another bowl, combine almond flour, oats, chopped walnuts, the remaining maple syrup, and coconut oil until crumbly.

4. Sprinkle the oat topping over the apples.
5. Bake for about 20-25 minutes until the topping is golden brown and the apples are tender.

6. Let it cool slightly before serving this delicious apple crisp.

Nutritional Value (Approximate):
Calories: 250, Carbohydrates: 30g, Protein: 4g, Fat: 13g, Fiber: 5g, Sugar: 15g

7-DAY MEAL PLAN

Day 1

Breakfast: Blueberry Oatmeal Smoothie

Snack: Apple Slices with Peanut Butter

Lunch: Quinoa and Vegetable Stir-Fry

Dinner: Roast Pumpkin Puree

Day 2

Breakfast: Blue Majik Pancakes

Snack: Sweet Potato Noodles with Cashew Sauce

Lunch: Turkey and Avocado Wrap

Dinner: Beef and Broccoli Stir-Fry

Day 3

Breakfast: Banana Walnut Muffins

Snack: Cottage Cheese and Pineapple

Lunch: Lentil Soup with Spinach

Dinner: Lentil & Vegetable Penne Pasta

Day 4

Breakfast: Avocado Breakfast Bowl

Snack: Mushroom and Red Kidney Bean Patties

Lunch: Salmon Salad with Lemon-Dill Dressing

Dinner: Vegetable Curry with Brown Rice

Day 5

Breakfast: Turkey and Cheese Sandwich

Snack: Rice Cake with Avocado and Tomato

Lunch: Chickpea and Tomato Stew

Dinner: Grilled Chicken with Mango Salsa

Day 6

Breakfast: Eggs, Sausage, and Whole-Grain Bread

Snack: Beetroot and Cashew Puree

Lunch: Chicken and Vegetable Skewers

Dinner: Eggplant Parmesan

Day 7

Breakfast: Scrambled Tofu with Vegetables
Snack: Almond Butter Energy Balls
Lunch: Tofu Salad with Sesame Ginger Dressing
Dinner: Shrimp and Vegetable Skewers

CONCLUSION

In concluding this Parkinson's disease diet cookbook for the newly diagnosed, it's essential to recognize the transformative power of nutrition in managing this condition. Through carefully curated recipes and dietary guidelines, this cookbook offers a practical and empowering approach to improving health and well-being for individuals grappling with Parkinson's.

By embracing the principles outlined in this cookbook, readers can take proactive steps towards managing their symptoms and enhancing their quality of life. The diverse array of recipes provides not only nourishment but also enjoyment, demonstrating that eating well can be both delicious and therapeutic.

Furthermore, the testimonials and success stories shared within these pages serve as a testament to the effectiveness of dietary interventions in managing Parkinson's disease. From improved motor function to enhanced cognitive clarity, the benefits of adopting a nutritious diet tailored to the needs of individuals with Parkinson's are undeniable.

As readers embark on their journey towards better health, it's important to remember that change takes time and patience. By incorporating the recipes and principles outlined in this cookbook into their daily lives, individuals can gradually cultivate healthier habits that support their overall well-being.

In closing, I encourage readers to approach this cookbook with an open mind and a willingness to explore new flavors and ingredients. By embracing the power of nutrition, individuals can take control of their health and embark on a path towards a brighter and more vibrant future, free from the constraints of Parkinson's disease.

BON APPETIT!!!

9 798324 565558